How growing brands can get u
and move forward with confi

# Radically Relevant

**Blake Howard**

Foreword by Alina Wheeler

For every brand leader who needs to
make a change but doesn't know how

# Table of Contents

Foreword — vi

Brand Basics — 2

The Value of Branding — 14

**Section 1**
How Radically Relevant Are You? — 20

**1.1**
What makes a great brand great? — 22

**1.2**
The Super Six — 30

**1.3**
Get your Radically Relevant score — 40

**Section 2**
Becoming More Radical — 48

**2.1 Clarity**
To be clear is to be kind — 54

**2.2 Distinction**
Hit 'em where they ain't — 66

**2.3 Control**
Hold on loosely — 74

**Section 3**
Becoming More Relevant                                      84

> **3.1 Attraction**
> Hey, good lookin'                                         88
>
> **3.2 Devotion**
> Keeping your brand's promises                             98
>
> **3.3 Alignment**
> All systems go                                           106

**Section 4**
What Now?                                                  114

Acknowledgments                                            126

About the Author                                           128

Endnotes                                                   129

# Foreword

Branding is a business imperative, regardless of your product, your service, or your size. Organizations across the public and private sector need to leverage their brands to gain a transcendent advantage in a fiercely competitive marketplace. Why? Because the best brands are powerful assets that attract new prospects, build trust, create lifelong customer relationships, and fuel employee engagement.

Perhaps your CEO has given you the daunting task of leading a new brand initiative. Perhaps your company has never invested in branding per se, and the leadership team is not convinced that a rebrand initiative has a measurable ROI. Having worked with hundreds of organizations, from Fortune 100 companies to start-ups and nonprofits, I believe the biggest universal challenge is getting the C-suite on the same page regarding brand strategy, execution, and capital investment.

Good news! *Radically Relevant* is the go-to guide you have been looking for. Blake Howard has created a user-friendly brand resource that will help you grow your brand, unify your team, and jump-start the branding process (with confidence). An experienced practitioner, Blake has worked with global heavy-hitters and ambitious start-ups to uncover and express what makes them unique. His firm, Matchstic, specializes in brand identity—helping clients seize every opportunity to fuel recognition, amplify differentiation, and be the brand of choice.

I have been following Matchstic's work for almost two decades, and I am a big fan of their approach to change management and their creative process. I am also a big fan of Blake's podcast, *A Change of Brand*. His interviews with brand and agency leaders reveal behind-the-scenes true stories that illuminate and engage.

Blake reminds us all that change takes courage, and that branding is a marathon, not a sprint. No one does it alone—bringing a brand to life each day and assuring its continued growth is hard work.

*Radically Relevant* provides you and your team with brand fundamentals and tangible, achievable advice presented in a friendly, easy-to-read format. The tools that Matchstic has developed and tested over the years are in this book and help make the complex simple.

What truly distinguishes *Radically Relevant* from hundreds of other branding resources, however, is an assessment tool that has a companion component on the web. Use this tool to see where your brand stands and where it needs to be. This framework does not replace an in-depth analysis, but it helps your team compare notes and gain insight into your brand strengths and branding effectiveness. More so, it helps you identify the key factors to increase brand engagement and jump-start your planning process.

Take the time to dive into this vital brand resource. Find new ways to delight customers, engage employees, and grow your brand equity. As George Eliot famously said, "It's never too late to be what you might have been." Think big and knock it out of the park. Start today.

*Alina Wheeler*

Author, *Designing Brand Identity: An Essential Guide for the Whole Branding Team*

# Radically
# Relevant

# Brand Basics
## Let's start at the start.

Once upon a time, a farmer worked hard and saved his money to buy a cow. That cow prospered and produced baby cows. Those cows also prospered and produced more cows.

Eventually, the farmer had an entire herd to feed, protect, and graze. He was a real cowboy. However, his neighbor was also a real cowboy, and her cows started to mix and blend in with the herd next door. Both farmers were greatly confused and didn't know whose property was whose. What's worse is that the neighbor had a neighbor, who was also a cowboy, and his cows mixed with the others.

Luckily, the farmers had the ancient Egyptians to look to for a solution.

Starting around 2700 B.C., the Egyptians began "branding" livestock, i.e., marking their animals with a specific symbol to identify ownership. These origins of the term "brand" give us insight into its relevance in our contemporary world. The (admittedly inhumane) practice of livestock branding was all about identification. Similarly, the purpose of branding today is to help consumers know who is who.

Today, organizational leaders know how important brand is for acheiving their strategic goals. But there's a misconception that, when your business reaches a certain size, you go out and create a brand. You hire the agency, workshop the tagline, pick one of three logos, and BOOM—there's your brand.

# Of course, it's much more complicated than that.

| A BRAND ISN'T… | A BRAND IS… |
|---|---|
| A one-off marketing project | Ongoing reputation-building |
| What you say about yourself | What others say about you |
| Your name, logo, or last ad campaign | The sum total experience of every touchpoint someone has with your organization |

# A brand isn't just a one-off marketing exercise; it's your company's reputation.

And it's being built slowly, over time, through the thousands of tiny touchpoints that customers and prospects have with your organization.

That reputation has the potential to swell over time into an undeniable competitive advantage. I like how Steve Jobs put it. He believed your brand was like a bank account with a long receipt of deposits (positive experiences) and withdrawals (negative experiences). The idea being to stay in the black.

**Signage**

**Buttery Croissants**

# Next door to my office is a cafe that makes you feel like you have stumbled into a little slice of Paris smack in the middle of Atlanta, Georgia.

This cafe, with sweet little bistro tables and pink and green floral wallpaper, serves the most amazing pastries. It's a feel-good experience, all the way through to that first bite of a buttery croissant. Your receipt even comes with a note at the bottom explaining a 4% upcharge that goes toward paying for employees' health insurance. (No wonder the bakers are so nice.) Never has it felt so good to overpay for coffee. From the bakers' aprons, down to the design of the coffee cups, every touchpoint reinforces the idea that you've stumbled into a French cafe in the middle of Atlanta, Georgia.

# Brand

- Table Markers
- Coffee Cups
- Aprons
- Tables
- Music
- Wallpaper
- Website
- Scent/Smell
- Payment Platform
- Service Style

It's one thing to make a boutique coffee shop feel magical. But what happens when this cafe expands to 10 locations across the Southeast? Or 100 across the country? Right now, the owner of my favorite coffee shop has complete control of the brand. So how does she make sure she grows the company in a way that stays true to her vision and doesn't turn into a mass-produced, sterile experience?

# Your brand is the sum total experience of every interaction someone has with you.

Radically Relevant

As your company grows, it must scale all of those interdependent complexities. It needs more employees to deliver the coffee with a smile, more dependable technology for seamless payment transactions, more interior design decisions, more social media posts, and so on. All of that can create a beautiful latte of chaos, inconsistency, and confusion.

Growing a brand is hard, and it's easy to get it wrong. Maybe you're not sure if you need to invest in your brand. Or maybe you are sure, but you're swimming upstream against a C-suite that's not easily convinced of its value. And even if that's not a challenge, you might still feel threatened by the growing number of competitors out there. (It's never been easier to start a business. In fact, the United States Patent and Trademark Office reports nearly 1 million trademarks filed per year.)[1]

What if there were an answer to help you move through this ambiguous swirling brand challenge? What would it look like to have your entire C-suite aligned on the essence of your brand? What if your creative team knew exactly what was on-brand and what wasn't? What if you acquired new customers left and right because you were clearly the right choice—and you could prove your brand was a valuable asset in achieving the company's vision?

These aren't silver-bullet hypotheticals. A Radically Relevant brand should do all of those things. An organization with a strong brand identity will grow and evolve without coming across as confused and unpredictable. A confident brand makes for confident employees, customers, and investors who are excited to join you on the journey.

When our clients are facing a brand change, more than anything they are looking for clarity and confidence on how to move forward. That's what this book provides. First, we'll talk about the basics of brand and what we call the Radically Relevant brand: the gold standard of where you want to be. Then you'll take an assessment that will help you plot your brand against the competition and pinpoint your strengths and weaknesses. Finally, you'll learn some practical tips for how to improve in six key areas in order to maximize your brand's effectiveness.

And it all begins in a packed arena with thousands of screaming toddlers.

# The Value of Branding

## What is a good brand worth?

You haven't lived until you've been to *Disney On Ice*.

I know, because we took all three of my kids a few years back at the height of the *Frozen* fanaticism taking the country by storm. They were over the moon to see Elsa. Skating. On ice. It was my first real foray into the world of Disney.

We hadn't yet made a family trip to Disney World, or gotten a Disney+ subscription, or traveled down the Walt wormhole (although we have achieved all those things now). And the moment we entered the arena, the magic was upon us. Fog machines whirred. Lights danced across our faces. Music boomed. And—never one to miss an upsell—Disney vendors strolled through the aisles selling licensed, "authentic" Elsa wands.

My daughter *really* wanted one. So as the kind and loving father I am, I waved the vendor over and asked the price. It was a cold, hard $25. This wand couldn't perform any actual magic. It was just twelve inches of cheap plastic. (Like I said, Disney newbie over here.) My daughter looked up at me with imploring eyes, and I considered how much I would spend on Amazon buying something virtually identical—probably for less than $2. But it wouldn't have the *Frozen* logo, and it wouldn't *feel* magical the way that one did in that exact moment, and it wouldn't make my daughter's eyes light up the way they did right then. The emotional value of a wand with a *Frozen* sticker, in an arena with an overly stimulated and sugar-filled three-year-old tugging on my shirt, far exceeded the functional value of the same product in a different context.

## We bought one for each kid.

Over and over again, organizations with a strong brand face less price pressure than those without one. We even see this in the nonprofit world. In 2021, Charity: Water, which puts enormous energy and talent behind its branding, raised over $100 million in revenue,[2] whereas Water.org raised a third of that amount.[3]

If you're the Water.org of your industry, don't worry. This book is for you. At Matchstic, the majority of our clients are what we call challenger brands: organizations looking to move beyond bootstrap or startup mode and really scale. If you're a challenger brand, you aren't the mainstay or market leader, and in some ways, the cards are stacked against you. But you have one big advantage going for you: While all eyes are on the leader of your industry, you have time to hone your brand and get it right before you're too big to change. And in many ways, you have the most to gain.

# "While all eyes are on the leader of your industry, you have time to hone your brand and get it right before you're too big to change."

## STAGES OF BRAND GROWTH

### Pioneer
**Stage 1**

In startup mode, you're still proving and testing. Expect many changes and pivots to come.

### Challenger
**Stage 2**

You've validated your core business and begun to build a strong customer base. New services and offerings are in the works as you seek new growth opportunities.

### Established
**Stage 3**

You've become the leader in many ways. Maintaining your strengths and innovating are top of mind.

### Legacy
**Stage 4**

The good ol' days might be behind you, but they're not forgotten. Maintaining new energy and relevance are required for continued success.

### Dying
**Stage 5**

After many years of success, you haven't adapted in time to keep up. It's time for a Hail Mary or an exit.

The challenger brands we talk with typically need help retelling their story. Maybe they've been focused on a single product or service. But now they're growing their offerings, which complicates the message.

Oftentimes, challenger brands are also looking for one or more of these things:

- Top-line growth
- To stand out in their competitive landscape
- More efficient and effective marketing efforts
- Brand strategy and architecture definition
- Internal alignment
- Industry recognition
- Successful recruitment of top talent

Sound familiar?

Of course, organizations like Disney and Charity: Water have invested a lot of time and resources into their brands. And an investment like that may frighten the higher-ups at your organization who hold the purse strings. But whether it's complex B2B technology or a cheap plastic wand, the perceived value of whatever you sell is inextricably linked to the strength of its brand.

# So, how valuable is your brand? Let's find out.

## Section 1
# How Radically Relevant Are You?

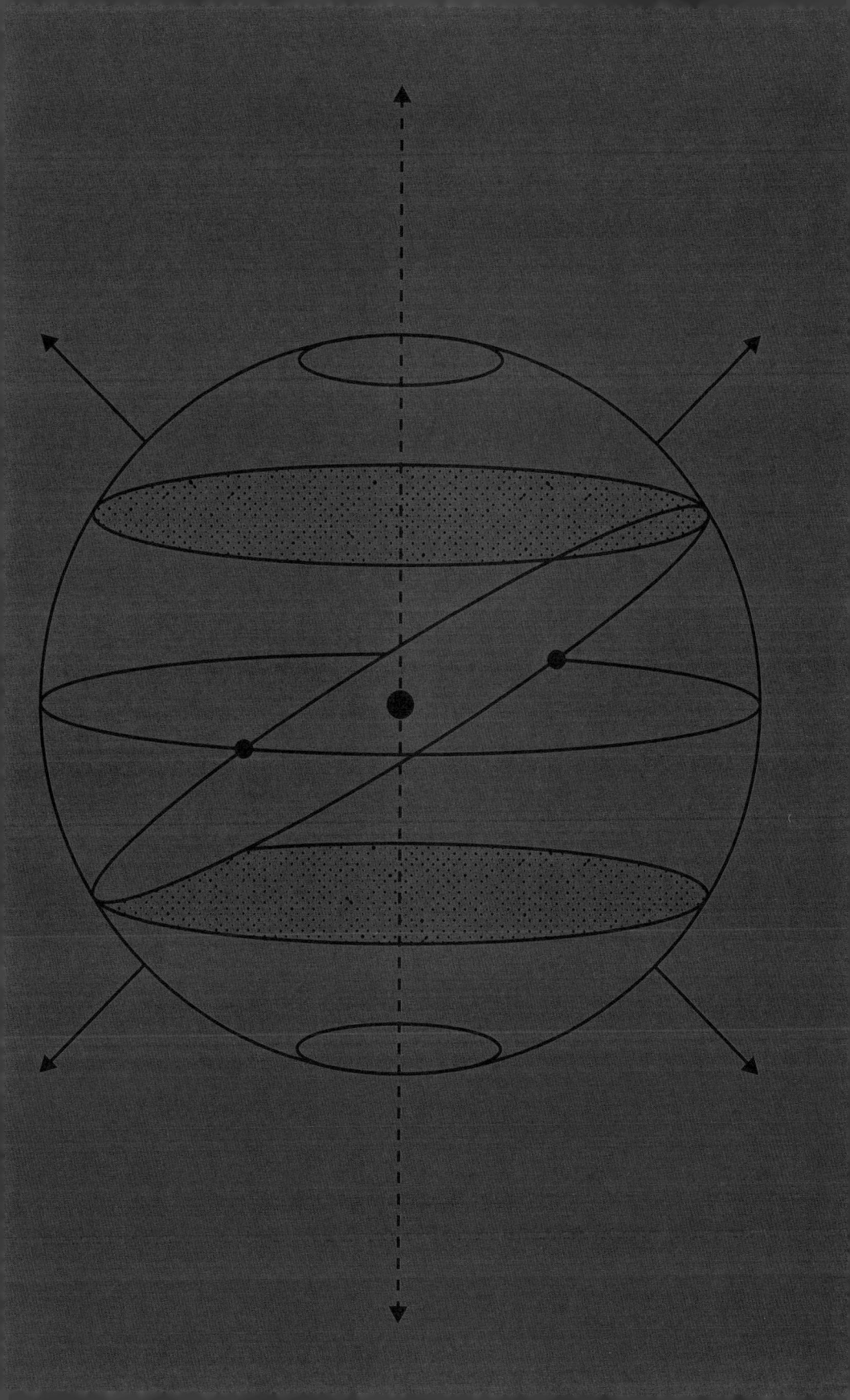

## 1.1
# What makes a great brand great?

This question stumps the most seasoned leader. And it turns out the answer is pretty simple. Great brands are both radical and relevant.

**Radical,** meaning they are unique and differentiated within their space.

**Relevant,** meaning they are relatable and valuable to their audience.

No matter your age or stage, you'll find yourself in one of these four categories in the Radically Relevant framework.

# OUTLAWS & OUTCASTS

# RADICALLY RELEVANT

**Radical**

# DATED & DYING

# COPYCAT

**Relevant**

How Radically Relevant Are You?

# Outlaws & Outcasts

These brands are on the bleeding edge of trends or technology, risking it all to be disruptive with a new idea. However, they are disconnected from or unaware of true audience needs and wants.

# Dated & Dying

Often, these are former leaders whose industries have been disrupted and offerings rendered irrelevant. They seem outdated and unaware of it, making no significant efforts to change.

# Radically Relevant

This is the holy grail of brands. Their offering, message, look, and feel are not only highly differentiated but also compelling and relevant to audiences—standing the test of time.

# Copycat

These are value-based brands driven by trends and price pressure. Their offerings are relevant but not unique, making them easily replaceable by the next company that can do it faster and cheaper.

Brands that score highly on the radical side have found their differentiation and are able to offer the market a highly unique product or service. Those that score highly on the relevant side of things have found a wide audience that values what they do. Those that forget to be either radical or relevant become, well, Blockbuster.

As an example of Outlaws & Outcasts, consider the clothing brand Vollebak, whose tagline is "clothes from the future." For just over a thousand dollars, you can have the Full Metal Jacket—built with 65% copper!

I actually think the Vollebak brand is pretty cool. It's gotten attention from *TIME* and other media outlets. And in Vollebak's own words, their goal is to "use science and technology to create clothing that no-one else can or will." Unashamed to follow its convictions and take bold actions, they've cut through the clutter by being totally over-the-top. The challenge now is, who's going to buy their products? When you're off-the-charts radical, you can sometimes alienate people. You may find your niche, but it will be too narrow of a market. They're missing the "relevant" piece.

At the opposite end of the spectrum is a value-based brand like Old Navy that is positioned completely around price. They're popular with their audience. But as a buyer, it doesn't really matter whether you get your $20 sweater from Old Navy or Amazon. Copycat brands have little to no audience devotion: The moment their offering is inconvenient or not priced right, buyers look elsewhere.

Similarly, have you ever bought anything from Wayfair? Of course you have. Do you remember who made the item? Of course you don't. Product brands on Wayfair are highly relevant in terms of price and style, but they don't carry customer awareness, devotion, or emotional connections. As soon as Thistle & Fig (what I imagine is the name of the ghost brand that made your Wayfair nightstand) stops having the best price or the fastest delivery, Wayfair will find someone else to source its nightstands. Copycat brands can often be very successful, but they're also replaceable. They're missing the "radical" piece.

Surprisingly few brands are both radical and relevant, and I think it's because they err in one of two directions:

1. They look so far inward that they miss seeing their audience's changing wants and needs. This leads to a lack of relevance.
2. They lack the courage to follow through on their convictions and instead resort to copycat behavior. This leads to a lack of radical distinction.

In 2014, Tesla, Inc., had developed game-changing technology for electric vehicles, but they were still losing the battle against gasoline-powered cars. Tesla was radical, but they weren't yet relevant. So they did something even more extreme: They gave away their patents. This allowed other car makers to produce electric vehicles, which meant fewer gas-powered cars on the road, fewer carbon emissions in the air, more charging stations being built, and more infrastructure to support electric vehicle drivers. Tesla made a strategic move to become more relevant—and it paid off. Since then, their market cap has increased by over 900%.[4]

Like Tesla, many challenger brands don't just seek to unseat the industry leader but to disrupt their entire industry. A Radically Relevant brand stands firm on its convictions and understands that the brand is built for the customer. It gets laser-focused on who they are, how they serve them, and the value they create.

## To be Radically Relevant, you have to deeply understand what makes you unique and what your customers want and need.

And then you have to find a way to show up in the world that will resonate with your audience.

It's no small task. So let's break it down into a few bite-sized chunks. Six to be exact.

## 1.2
# The Super Six

There are six categories that make a brand Radically Relevant. They've remained steadfast and critical, proven time and time again. We'll spend the rest of the book expanding on these in more detail, but before you take the assessment, here's a quick overview:

## RADICAL

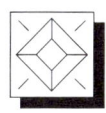

### CLARITY
The ability to be clearly and easily understood

### DISTINCTION
The ability to dramatically stand out from your direct competitors

### CONTROL
The ability to produce consistent communications and experiences

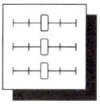

## RELEVANT

### ATTRACTION
The ability to draw in new, ideal audiences

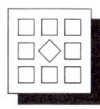

### DEVOTION
The ability to consistently deliver on your promises

### ALIGNMENT
The ability for everyone in your organization to be in sync on your brand story and values

# Clarity

## The ability to be clearly and easily understood.

The last time you were at a cocktail party and someone asked you what you did for a living, did they respond meaningfully when you told them? Or did their eyes glaze over?

Older, more established industries typically do well in the clarity category. For example, restaurants, security companies, and law firms don't usually have to explain what they do. But new categories and innovators will need to work harder to clarify their offering.

Clarity is important for obvious reasons: If someone doesn't understand what you sell, why would they buy it?

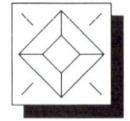

# Distinction

## The ability to dramatically stand out from your direct competitors.

Has your company ever been confused with a competitor?

Distinction isn't about being different from any other brand out there, but about standing out on your competitive playground. Look around. Does everyone in your industry use the term "integrated solutions" or have blue as their brand color? As the famous baseball player, Willie Keeler, said, "Hit 'em where they ain't." Look for the holes in your competitive landscape and be decidedly different. Where are the unoccupied areas no one else has gotten to yet that you can own—whether that's in your message, color, or positioning?

# Control

## The ability to produce consistent communications and experiences.

Have you ever scrolled your Instagram feed and felt like the posts could have come from five different organizations? Does your marketing team end up creating a new look for every new initiative, none of which really connect to one another? Do you catch the sales team constantly going rogue?

Brands can increase revenue by up to 23% just by showing up consistently in the world.[5] Oftentimes, a brand that is visually and verbally coherent across all touchpoints is the result of internal governance and systems. Translation: If you want your brand to be recognized by your target audience, you've got to become a bit of a control freak—as well as empower them with training, understanding, and tools.

# Attraction

## The ability to draw in new, ideal audiences.

If your brand were a storefront, would it lure shoppers in as they passed by? Would it be so compelling they'd be unable to resist entering? Or would they keep walking, judging it outdated and not for them?

Attraction starts by understanding what is valuable, needed, and interesting to your audience. In fact, a common mistake organizations make is spending too much time talking about themselves and what they offer, and too little time talking to their audience and what *they* need.

Rather than framing yourself as the hero, how can you frame your audience as the hero? Once they see you as someone who can help them on their own journey of greatness, attraction clicks.

# Devotion

## The ability to consistently deliver on your promises.

Once you've attracted a customer inside your store, do they stay there? Or do they sneak out the door the second you turn your back?

Devotion is perhaps the most important of the Super Six, because it's the key to customer loyalty. We all know how much easier and cheaper it is to keep an existing customer than to win a new one.

As my dad always says, "You can't put lipstick on a pig." It doesn't matter how many customers you attract. If your organization doesn't follow through on its promises, those customers will flow right out the back door.

# **Alignment**

## The ability for everyone in your organization to be in sync on your brand story and values.

Quick: What does your organization stand for? If you had to pull up a PowerPoint to answer this question—or run out into the office hallway to read the mission statement from a plaque—your organization may be missing alignment.

Alignment refers to the relevance of your brand internally. It is the unsung hero of the Super Six. As we said at the beginning, your brand isn't just your design and messaging, but your operations, customer service, and product development too. If those elements aren't aligned, we end up with the lipstick-on-the-pig scenario.

Think about it: How can your employees and leadership deliver on your brand promises if they don't know what they are?

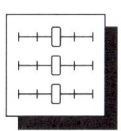

When these six factors are strong, they can be a positive, tailwind-driving force for the organization—increasing engagement, sales, and impact. On the other hand, if your Super Six are weak or nonexistent, they can act as a headwind hardship—muffling your impact and stalling your success.

# So, ready to find out where you stand?

## 1.3
# Get your Radically Relevant score

If you're like me, you've probably already been plotting your brand on the Radically Relevant scale, maybe cringing a little as you realize the areas where you may be falling short.

Instead of leaving you to act based on false assumptions and wrong hunches, we decided to create a quick but meaningful way to check your brand's effectiveness.

To get your Super Six score, navigate to the URL below. It takes only a few minutes to complete.

## RadicallyRelevantBrand.com

The purpose of this assessment is to provide a quick gut check, not to replace thorough market research. We recommend following up with a deeper dive to validate audience and employee perceptions.

After all, this book isn't meant to be the sole driver of a huge rebranding effort for a company with a lot to lose. Rather, it's meant to help you understand generally where you are in terms of your brand's strengths and to identify some practical action items for moving forward.

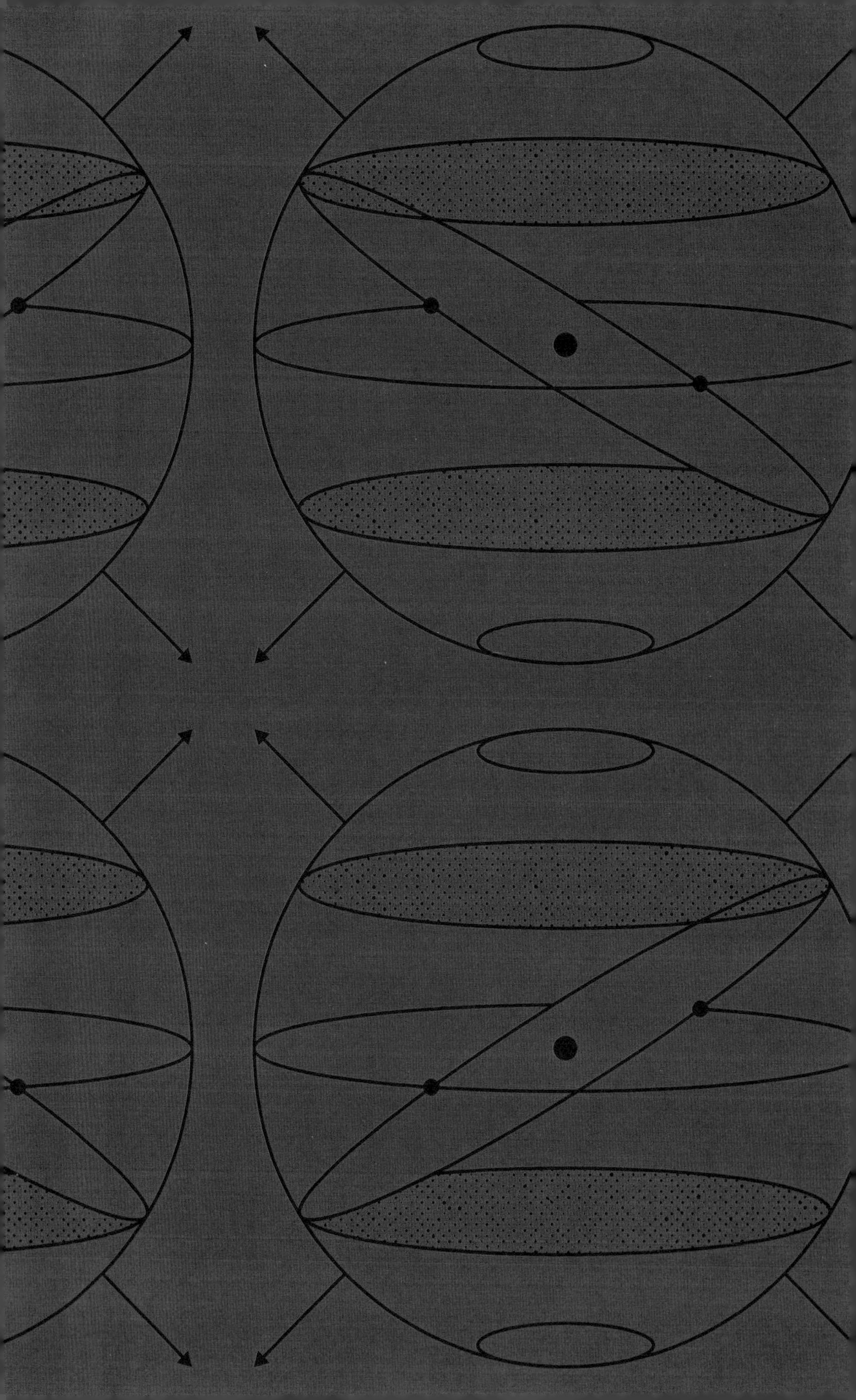

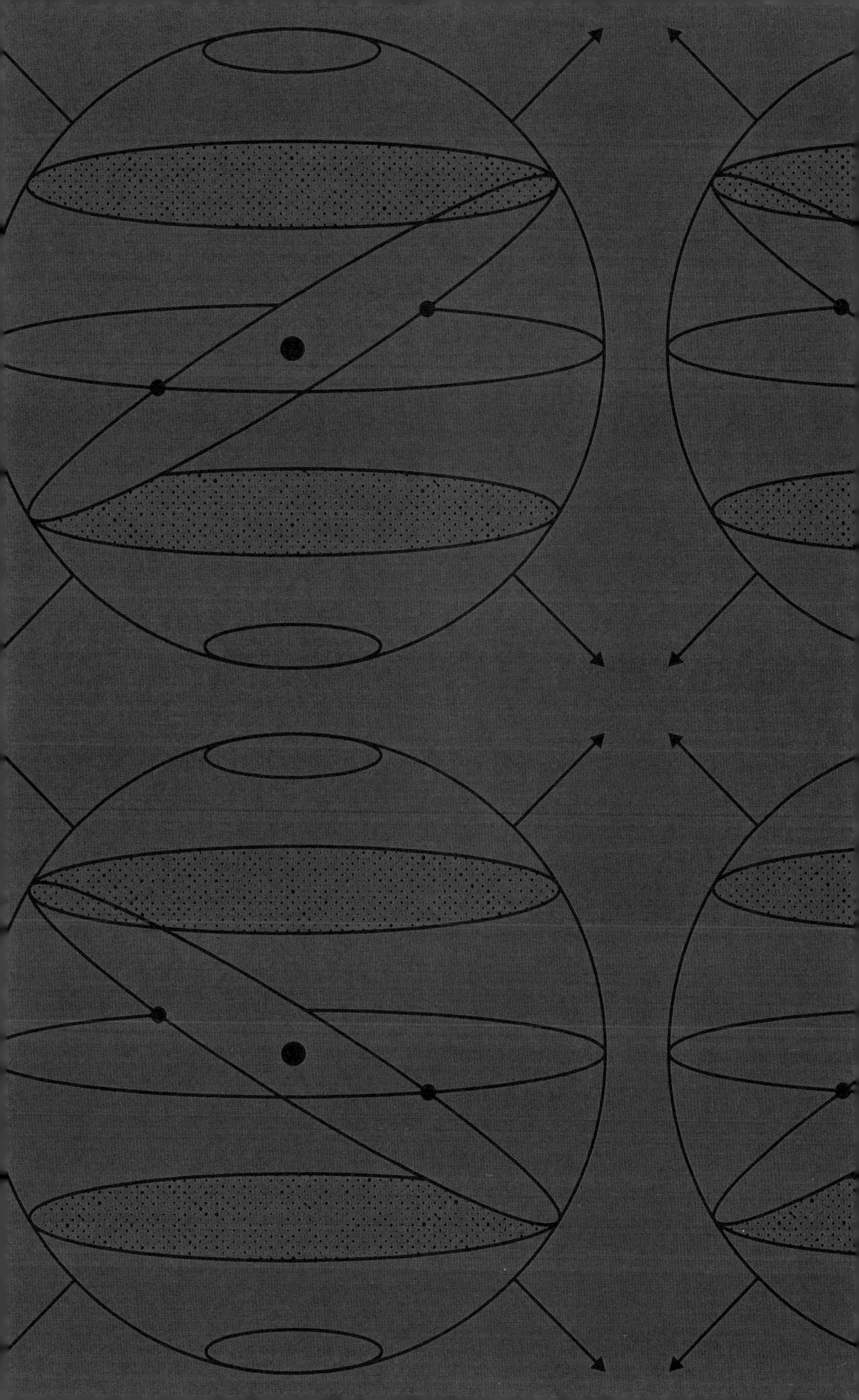

Are you back, score in hand? How did you do? Now you can check your scores against the guide below to better understand what they mean.

# Clarity

**(+)** A score of 51% or above here suggests a clear offering and intuitive brand or product architecture. Clarity is often found in mature, well-defined markets or categories. These brands are easy for audiences to understand, consider, and engage with.

**(–)** A score of 50% or below suggests audiences may have a limited understanding of your offerings or even be confused about your category altogether. It may indicate complicated relationships between your sub-brands or products. (Spoiler: Not everything deserves a logo.) Low-clarity brands typically require long-winded explanations in sales and marketing, which may only create further barriers for engagement. Low clarity is often found in emerging markets, scaling and growing brands, merger and acquisition scenarios, or organizations with a lack of focus.

# Distinction

**(+)** A score of 51% or above for distinction suggests you have a differentiated offering or experience, and conveys uniqueness through your name, message, logo, or look and feel, as compared to direct competitors. High-distinction brands tend to visually and verbally stand out in the marketplace and get more attention.

**(–)** A score of 50% or below suggests your brand may be expressing considerable sameness in the categories above. Low-distinction brands are often forgettable and even invisible to target audiences. Sometimes, entire categories can be full of low-distinction brands. In those industries, price or convenience typically wins out.

# Control

**(+)** A score of 51% or above here suggests your brand has consistent visual treatments (color, layout, type, imagery, etc.) and/or a consistent brand voice and message across multiple touchpoints. High-control brands are easily recognized by their audience. They provide a familiar and predictable experience, which builds trust and credibility.

**(–)** A score of 50% or below suggests an inconsistent and fragmented approach to brand communications. For example, you may be inconsistent with your use of color, type, image treatment, brand voice, product claims, message, etc. Low-control brands often inadvertently make skeptics of their prospects during the buying process, because their unpredictability creates a subconscious lack of trust in the brand.

# Attraction

**(+)** A score of 51% or higher for attraction suggests your brand is making a compelling first impression on your audience. High-attraction brands tend to see high growth in their marketing and sales metrics, as indicated by conversions, leads, opportunities, and/or increasing social and digital traffic.

**(–)** A score of 50% or lower for attraction suggests the brand is not instantly connecting with your audience. This could be due to an outdated or unappealing message and look, or simply one that isn't speaking to the full value you provide. Low-attraction brands are often legacy organizations that have long relied on relationships and word-of-mouth for new business. Consumers may describe them as dated or irrelevant.

# Devotion

**(+)** A score of 51% or above for devotion suggests your brand provides a valuable experience that keeps audiences engaged and coming back. High-devotion brands consistently deliver on their customers' expectations, having successfully operationalized their brand positioning throughout the organization. Because of devotion, these beloved brands often enjoy the privilege of premium pricing.

**(–)** A score of 50% or below for devotion suggests a lack of brand loyalty and high churn rate, often due to customer expectations not being met. Low-devotion brands struggle to establish long-term value in the minds of their customers and face intense price pressure from competitors.

# **Alignment**

**(+)** A score of 51% or above for alignment suggests your leadership has successfully defined and socialized a compelling brand strategy. They've made it clear how each area of the organization is expected to deliver on the brand—and with buy-in from higher-ups, those teams are held accountable through related performance indicators. High-alignment brands respect and understand the power of brand in today's marketplace, and thereby benefit from streamlined creative processes and cultural unity.

**(−)** A score of 50% or below for alignment suggests a lack of internal unity around the story the brand should tell in the market. Similar to low-control brands, low-alignment brands often project a fragmented image to their audiences, eroding trust. They also may suffer from inefficient internal brand processes, duplicate work, creative frustration, and general wheel-spinning.

## WHAT NOW?

If you scored high in all of the categories above, congratulations! You're a Radically Relevant brand. But if, like most organizations, you had low scores in a few of the categories, don't despair. We're about to look at what you can do next.

## Section 2
# Becoming More Radical

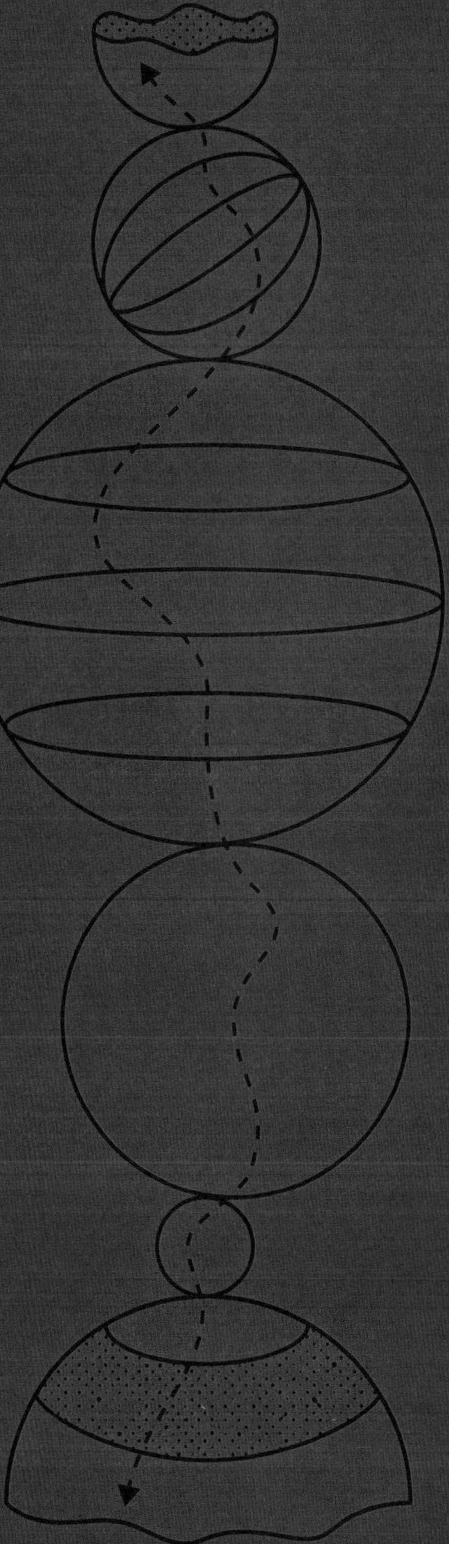

On Black Friday, 2011, the clothing brand Patagonia took
out a full-page ad in *The New York Times* with the headline,

# DON'T
# THIS J

**BUY**
**CKET**

# Telling consumers to not buy your product is a pretty bold move.

But Patagonia was acting on its values, which include sustainability and anti-consumerism—radical in itself for the apparel industry. The ad was both attention-grabbing and memorable, as witnessed by the fact that we're still talking about it more than a decade later.

(Patagonia has also consistently topped reputation rankings—a rare feat for clothing brands.)[6]

People love brands that make radical moves—the ones that are full of idiosyncrasies, unable to be anything other than their authentic selves, and unashamed to follow through on their convictions. Perhaps we love them because they unapologetically believe in what they're doing, and they're willing to break the rules to follow their convictions.

Radical tactics like the "Don't Buy This Jacket" ad above can help a brand connect with its audience. Being "in" on the joke makes people feel smarter, better, or more noble-minded, allowing brands to cut through the clutter and stand out among their peers.

Brands looking to be more radical take bold actions— not only with their marketing messages and visuals, but sometimes with their service models as well. In fact, they're often working to disrupt entire categories. They're out in the limelight, giving it their all, unafraid to fail or look stupid. They act like they have nothing to lose. And something in us can't help rooting for them. To break through the noise and stand out in your space, you have to get a little radical, especially if you're a Stage 1 (pioneering) brand.

## But what if you're not the Patagonia of your industry?

In the last chapter's assessment, you ranked your brand's (1) Clarity, (2) Distinction, and (3) Control. This half of the Super Six determines how radical your brand is. But there's good news: No matter how you scored on each of them, there's hope for your brand to become radical.

## 2.1
# To be clear is to be kind

**CREATING BRAND CLARITY**

Imagine you're at a big party, full of people, some you know, some you don't. Let's call it a wedding. An outdoor wedding. For your… cousin's daughter. Your favorite cousin.

The sun is shining, and there's a cool breeze. When out of nowhere, someone comes up to you and starts talking. This isn't just anyone. It happens to be your company's ideal customer. Someone with the potential to land you your biggest deal ever. They just don't know it yet. But then, finally, they utter the five words you've been waiting for: "So, what do you do?"

What *do* you do? The Motown music that the deejay is playing is loud, and you left your laptop with your PowerPoint on it in the car. You start to sweat, as you rattle on about this and that, dancing around your point but never quite landing it. Slowly, the stranger's eyes start to glaze over, and before you know it, they've excused themselves for the restroom, never to be seen again.

Clarity matters. And we've all struggled with it. But if your target audience can't understand what you do, they'll never understand what makes you great. To be more radical, you must first be clear. So, as Ricky Ricardo would say, "You've got some 'splainin' to do."

When it comes to brand clarity, it all comes down to two directions: You can paddle with the current by embracing the closest associated category and defining your differentiation within it. Or you can paddle against the current by creating an entirely new category. I typically urge people to go with option one. While it's tempting to think that what you offer is so drastically different from what's out there that you need exciting new language to describe yourself ("It's like Airbnb for fintech staffing!"), inventing a new category is an uphill battle. And you'll find yourself having to explain yourself over and over again.

# "...it's a mistake to sacrifice clarity on the altar of distinction."

Right now you're going, "But Blake, you said we need to be different! Isn't that what being radical is all about?" I know, my friend, I know. But I really think it's a mistake to sacrifice clarity on the altar of distinction. Distinction is still super important, but we'll get to that in the next chapter.

Take Matchstic, for example. It isn't easy to explain what we do. If we had called ourselves a "creative services agency," we would have put ourselves in the same category as much larger and more general firms. But if we had said we were a logo shop, we wouldn't have been able to expand into strategy, messaging, and naming. Ultimately, we decided to describe ourselves as a "brand identity house," which has allowed us to grow without becoming so broad as to be meaningless.

That first phrase that comes out of your mouth when someone asks what your company does? We call it your "first noun." You want your first noun to be more relatable than interesting. People need a frame of reference, and you can't be all things to all people. Get specific. Ambiguity is hard to grasp and easy to forget.

| TOO GENERIC | JUST RIGHT | TOO SPECIFIC |
| --- | --- | --- |
| Global NGO | Skilled Experts Fighting Oppression | Refugee Asylum Technologist |
| HR Hiring Platform | High-Volume Hourly Hiring Solution | SMS Applicant System |
| Scientists and Researchers | Water Technologists | Smart Water Bottle Manufacturer |

Think about it: Amazon didn't launch as the website where you could get anything under the sun delivered to your door. They were e-commerce for books. Nest started as the only smart thermostat, then grew to become a smart home brand. Square began as a payment terminal for small businesses, then expanded into a full-service financial solutions provider. Dropbox started as easy-to-use cloud storage for creatives, and is now competing with Microsoft and Google by offering word processing and other products for working professionals. You know who took the opposite approach and started out generic, broad, and lacked focus in their brand? Yeah, me neither—because we've never heard of them.

Land, then expand.[7] Choose a first noun that is specific, but not limiting; meaningful, but relatable. Get that right, and you're well on your way to brand clarity.

# We are a _____.

Radically Relevant

If you struggle with brand clarity, consider using a descriptive word in your tagline or core message. This doesn't mean you have to be completely uncreative. In fact, some core messages are both descriptive and emotional. Consider Delta ("Keep Climbing") or The Container Store ("Contain Yourself").

We once worked with a B2B technology company that provided a seamless checkout experience for e-commerce companies. There was a lot of confusion around what they did, so we came up with the core message, "Checkout without limits." It allowed us to use their first noun as an anchor word to clue people into what they did, while still adding plenty of personality and emotion.

# One area that can drive down clarity is brand architecture.

Too often, organizations make the mistake of branding their org chart instead of thinking about their offerings from their customers' point of view. But not every new product or service deserves a logo. In fact, new brands should exist only if they offer a distinct value proposition or exist in a unique category from the parent brand. Try using this decision tree the next time you roll out a new offering…

# So you want to launch a new brand or product?

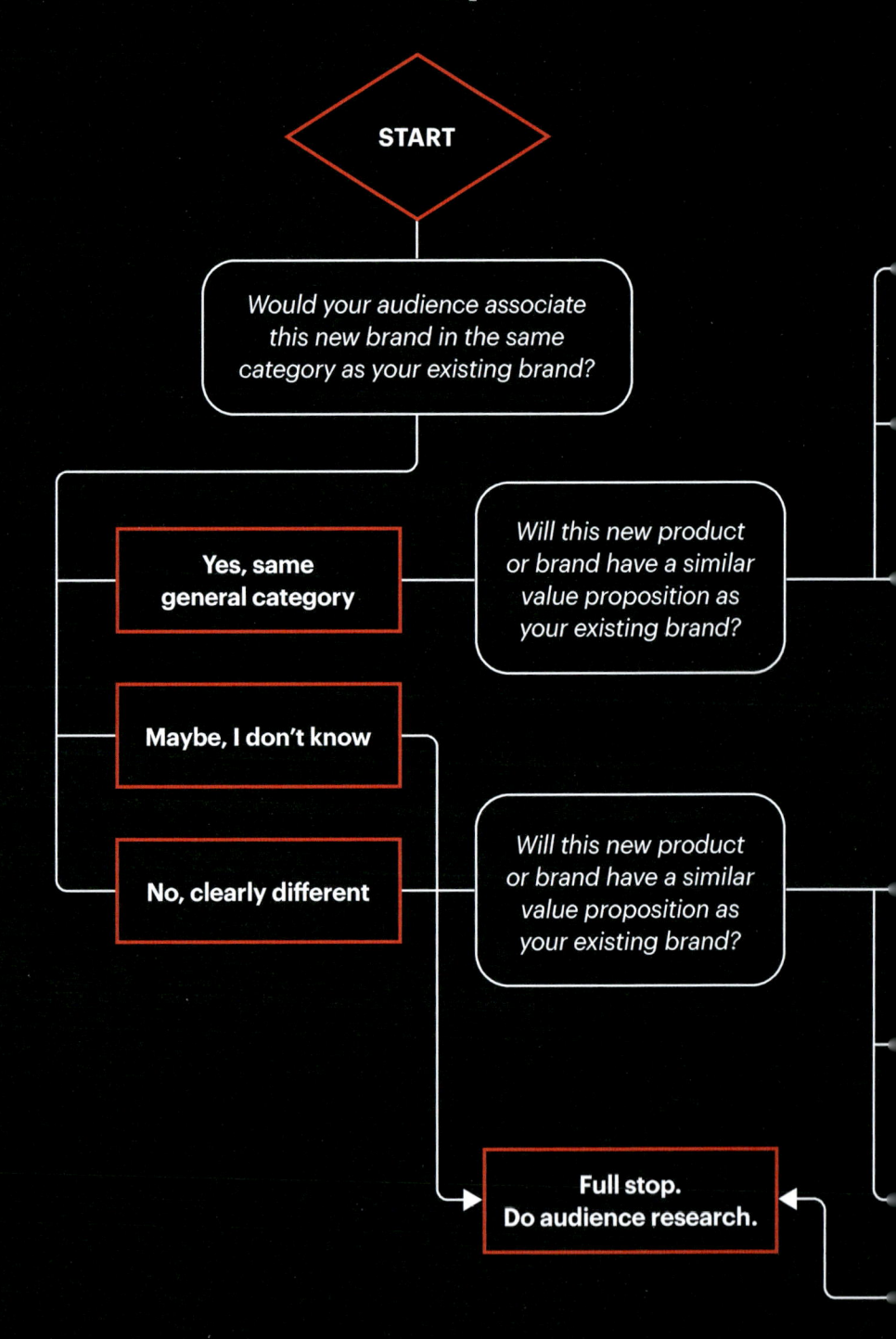

**START**

Would your audience associate this new brand in the same category as your existing brand?

- **Yes, same general category** → Will this new product or brand have a similar value proposition as your existing brand?
- **Maybe, I don't know**
- **No, clearly different** → Will this new product or brand have a similar value proposition as your existing brand?

**Full stop. Do audience research.**

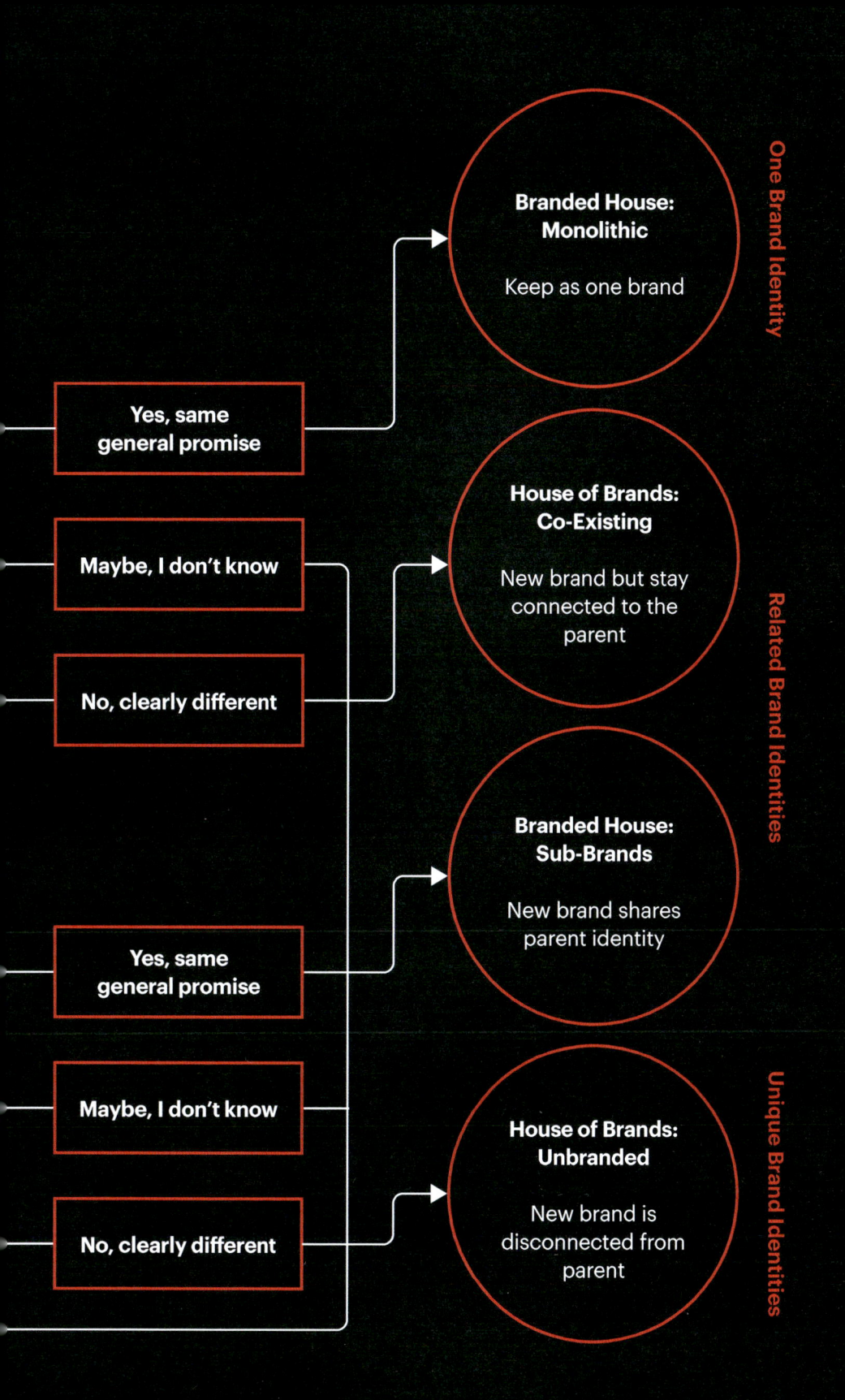

| Decision | Outcome | Category |
|---|---|---|
| **Yes, same general promise** | **Branded House: Monolithic** — Keep as one brand | One Brand Identity |
| **Maybe, I don't know** / **No, clearly different** | **House of Brands: Co-Existing** — New brand but stay connected to the parent | Related Brand Identities |
| **Yes, same general promise** | **Branded House: Sub-Brands** — New brand shares parent identity | Related Brand Identities |
| **Maybe, I don't know** / **No, clearly different** | **House of Brands: Unbranded** — New brand is disconnected from parent | Unique Brand Identities |

# More Ways to Be Clear and Kind

❑ Does your messaging depend on broad, vague terms—or ones with meaning? See if you can get more specific, even if it feels a bit limiting.

❑ If you are in an emerging technology or complex business, and/or your brand name says nothing about what you do, consider injecting some descriptive language into your core message.

- ❏ Organize your offerings in a way that is meaningful to your audience, not internal politics or territorial org charts.

- ❏ Look deeper at your existing portfolio of brands (if applicable). Do they all offer unique value, or are some redundant? Where can you simplify?

# 2.2
# Hit 'em where they ain't

**CREATING BRAND DISTINCTION**

Now that we've talked about clarity, it's time to talk about being distinct within the category you've placed yourself. This is one reason specificity is important: The bigger your category, the more noise there is to cut through.

Now, more than ever, consumers have more choices—and you have more competition. If clarity is all about your first noun, positioning is all about your area of differentiation. Here's a simple framework[8] you can use to carve that out:

# We are the

*[first noun category]*

---

# that

*[area of distinction]*

---

If you look around at your competitive playground, you're sure to find some elbow room for distinction. Where do your competitors lack that you excel? Do you have a stronger product? Deeper knowledge and expertise? Higher speed and efficiency? And before you say, "(d) all of the above!" know that when your audience hears that, what they remember is, "(e) none of the above." So choose just one thing you want people to remember you for, and laser-focus on it. Apple has great customer service, but when it comes to marketing their products, they're not spending expensive air time talking about their Genius Bar—they're showing you a big, drool-inducing photo of the latest iPhone.

# "Being authentic is better than being different but fake."

Of course, Apple can only hang its hat on product quality because they have decades of strong products to stand behind. So whatever area of distinction you choose, make sure it's something you can truly deliver on. Customers can smell B.S. from a mile away. Being authentic is better than being different but fake. And to paraphrase something a client recently said to me, no one wants a branding comb over.

You should err on the side of authenticity, but sometimes your competitive set gives you an opportunity. Why did Kubota tractors choose orange? Because John Deere is green. Why did Lyft choose pink? Because Uber is black. If you've looked around at your competitors, and there really aren't any areas where you're noticeably better than they are, you can always look to personality to create distinction.

For decades, bottled water companies have been coming up with new ways to get people to pay for something you can get for free from your kitchen faucet. In the 1990s, evian spun a unique story around the source of their water, turning it into a status symbol that became popular with celebrities. In the early 2000s, smartwater marketed the concept of electrolytes and made bottled water more accessible with modern design, quirky copy, and lowercase letters. In the 2010s, Voss got creative with packaging and introduced a sleek cylindrical bottle that coordinated perfectly with yoga pants. Today, LIFEWTR uses their labels to showcase colorful designs from a series of artists, making the bottles feel like collectibles. Along the way, there's also been boxed water, canned water, and even something called Liquid Death (tagline: "Murder Your Thirst"). Whether it's colorful artwork, unique stories, or wild names, in a crowded or commoditized category like water, you'll have to leverage your unique personality in order to stand out.

Also consider a brand called Welly. For decades, the first-aid industry was dominated by a single player—so much so that "Band-Aid" became a more commonly used term than the generic "bandage." But then came 2017, and Welly Bravery Badges. The product is essentially identical to Band-Aids, but instead of being flesh-colored, the bandages come in fun colors and patterns and are packaged in cute, reusable tins. Welly's VP of Marketing explained, "[The founders] saw opportunities to combine premium materials with bright colors and bold designs to reach an audience that is ready to embrace their cuts and scrapes as badges of a life well lived."[9]

Welly's positioning might look something like this:

## We are the **first aid company** that **celebrates bumps and scrapes instead of hiding them.**

Personality as distinction isn't just for consumer brands; it works in B2B as well. At Matchstic, I once worked with a laminate company that bought their materials from the same wholesale manufacturers as everyone else in their industry. It was just the way the industry worked: Everyone sold the exact same product. So we designed a brand that was the most artful and sophisticated in the space, in order to attract interior designers. Their brand personality became their distinction.

Similarly, when the email marketing company Mailchimp started, there were already several other email automation platforms that essentially did the exact same thing. But Mailchimp's competitors were utilitarian and vanilla. In a word: boring. So Mailchimp differentiated itself by going all in on personality. If you typed "asteroids" into their website's search bar, the page would transform into a video game. As you were about to publish your newsletter, their monkey mascot's sweaty finger would hover over the "send" button. When you finally did hit send, the monkey would high-five you in celebration. Mailchimp had realized something important: They could take a dry piece of technology and turn it into the best part of someone's day. Why choose vanilla when you could have rainbow sprinkles? Mailchimp's audience of graphic designers, entrepreneurs, and marketing professionals ate it right up.[10]

Mailchimp's positioning at the time might have looked something like this:

We are the **email automation platform** that **deeply understands and delights our users.**

# Amp Up Your Brand's Personality

❏ If you're selling a physical product, what's your signature brand moment? (Think of Tiffany & Co.'s blue box, Maker's Mark's red wax seal, or Apple's perfectly engineered white packaging.)

❏ Is everyone talking about their capabilities with the same industry jargon and cliches? Message your benefits with language that's totally different.

❏ Are your competitors all clustered in one corner of the brand color wheel? Make a splash with a bold color choice.

❏ Is everyone stuck on stock photography? Spring for a custom photoshoot or hire an illustrator.

❏ Seeing the same basic geometric sans serif typeface everywhere? Use a different one to send a not-so-subtle message that you're unique.

# 2.3
# Hold on loosely

**CREATING BRAND CONTROL**

## No one wants to sow distrust in a prospect or give off amateur vibes.

But social media posts that are visually all over the place or communications using every font under the sun will do just that. Anyone looking to grow into a market leader will need a consistent message—a look and feel that your audience recognizes to be you.

Therefore, the goal of brand control isn't to scratch some creative director's OCD itch (guilty). Rather, it's to put a consistent brand presence into the market. And, hey, I get it. Nobody wants to be the brand police. Nobody wants to be brand-policed, either. Yet too often, brand guidelines are strict and legalistic, extinguishing creativity instead of igniting it—like handcuffs used to restrain content creators. They've understandably gotten a bad rap.

But on the other hand, when there's little control of the brand, your assets end up all over the place. This tends to happen when the brand exists only in someone's head— maybe the founder or original marketing hire. As the organization scales—adding team members and new products and capabilities—people get confused about what's on brand and what isn't, left with little more than their subjective opinions to lead them back on track.

*Consistently presented brands are about 3.5 times more likely to enjoy excellent brand visibility than those with an inconsistent brand presentation.*[11]

# What's a brand to do?

The trick is to create the right level of definition, where brand guidelines don't stifle creativity, but they aren't the Wild West, either. They should give your creative team inspiration, not limitation. They should act like a trampoline your people can bounce off of, and that will be there to catch them if they fall.

Look at Spotify. They've found a way to present a consistent visual language, even though they have 82 million tracks and more than 4 million podcasts. They use color, image overlays, and plenty of restraint to organize the playlist chaos.

At Matchstic, we typically work with clients to develop a set of personality attributes, in addition to the positioning framework discussed earlier. These attributes bring direction to specific visual and verbal tactics that help in-house designers, writers, and marketers exercise their creativity without putting something out into the world that feels disconnected from the rest of the brand.

Here's an example of brand attributes we developed for an international humanitarian NGO:

## NGO BRAND ATTRIBUTES

## Hopeful

We have a vision for a brighter world. Our tone of voice does not dwell on the problems, but boldly shares our solutions.

## Principled

We are not known for one brand color; we are more subtle, nuanced, and inclusive, with many shades and perspectives, like those we fight for.

## Poised

We create layouts with elegant simplicity and design details that represent our quiet confidence.

## Tenacious

We speak with bold convictions and raw determination.

## Seasonsed

With 40 years of history, we honor our legacy, but we keep moving forward.

"Typically, people run off the rails because they're in a hurry, or they don't know where to find the resources."

It can be helpful to think of your brand as having a kit of parts. This kit includes everything from your name and logo to the brand voice your content team uses to write your web copy and social media posts, the typographic system and colors your designers create your ads with, and more. You can arm a franchise owner or head of marketing with this kit, and suddenly they have the tools they need to make brand magic—and not brand mishaps.

One framework we've found helpful is the "this or that" exercise. Maybe your brand is humorous, but not slapstick; clever, but not snarky; friendly, but not casual. Guardrails like these can help keep content creators from going rogue.

For example:

## WE SOUND...

**Driven, not overbearing**
**Expert, not academic**
**Sincere, not too serious**
**Inviting, but professional**

No one *wants* to be off-brand. Typically, people run off the rails because they're in a hurry, or they don't know where to find the right resources. If you can do some of the work for them—equipping them with clear boundaries and frameworks to operate within—they'll happily stay in your lanes.

# Tightening the Reins on Brand Control

❑ **Record a video.** Use a technology like Loom to record yourself explaining the brand, what it stands for, where the guardrails are, and who to go to with questions. Make the video part of employee onboarding.

❑ **Start a "Brand School"** for creatives or agencies. Coach them on color usage, logo placement, typography, voice, etc., and walk them through best practices for each. Start it during employee orientation and repeat quarterly or biannually to create a regular rhythm.

- **Hold a brand voice workshop.** Invite anyone who writes or speaks on behalf of your brand, including fundraisers, sales people, retail staff, freelance copywriters, etc. Explain the brand voice, as well as your key messaging elements. Have them put the messaging into practice. Hold space for questions.

- **Perform quarterly or annual brand audits.** Print or pin up a collection of materials. Do they look like they're coming from the same place?

❑ **Create templates** for common assets that need to be created frequently, such as monthly newsletters, promotional emails, social media posts, or even customer service calls. That way, you control the scaffolding, while letting creators play within it.

❑ **Use technology platforms** to house interactive and easy-to-use guidelines, as well as the most up-to-date templates and brand assets.

❑ **Appoint a Brand Governor.** Rather than someone who's going to blow the whistle on every minor infraction, select someone who can act more like a point person for questions that people may have about the brand. Make it part of their job description and quarterly responsibilities to create helpful frameworks and tools for brand ambassadors to use.

## Section 3
# Becoming More Relevant

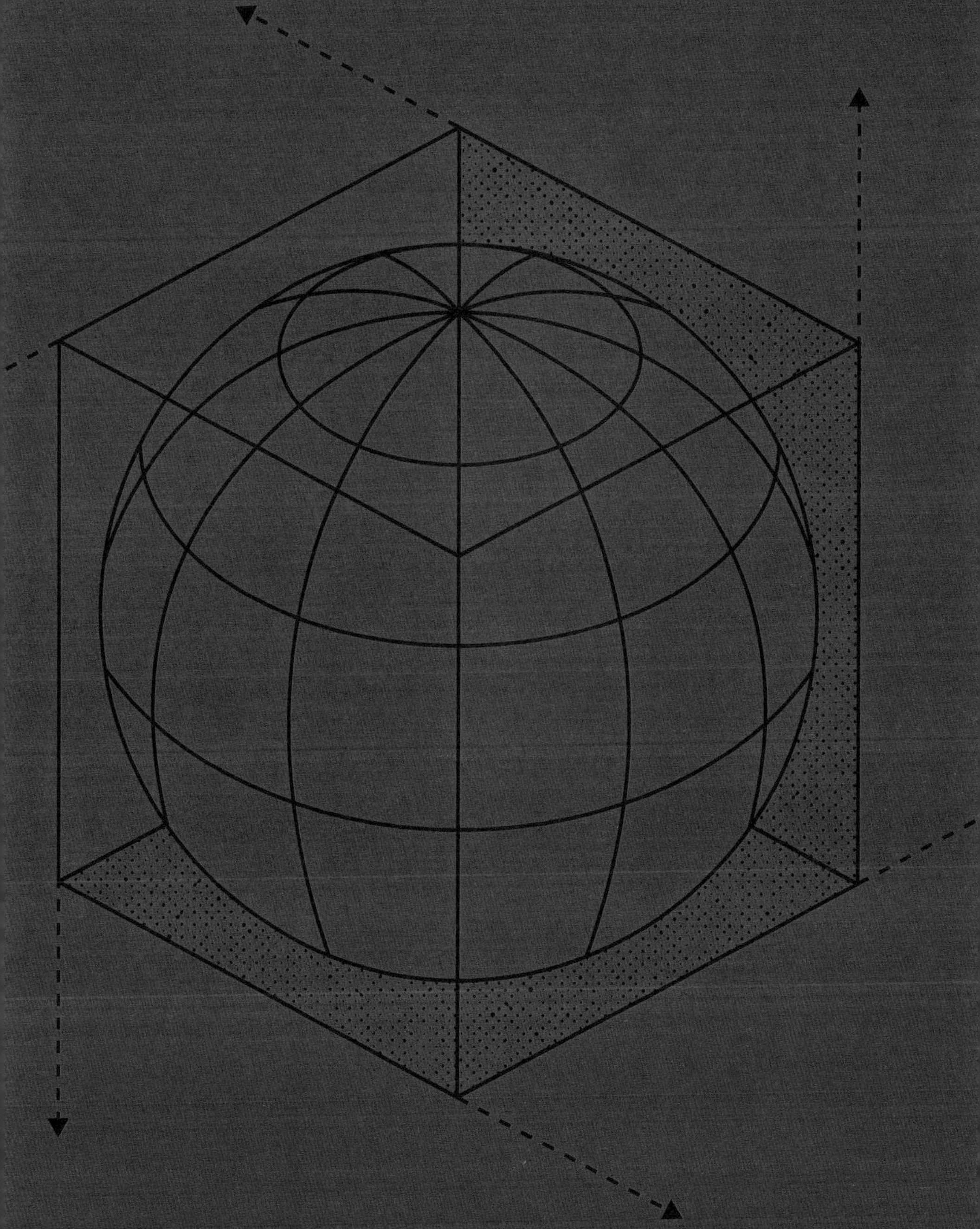

# It's

Can you believe that? Your brand isn't about your personal preferences, how cool your offerings are, or if you have a ping-pong table in the break room. It exists for your audience alone.

You could easily get this far, create a brand that is radical, and it could all be an exercise in vanity. Because at the end of the day, none of this is about you. It's about the audience your brand serves. Think about it: No one likes that guy at the cocktail party who wants to talk only about himself. The most successful brands speak to a very specific audience with very specific needs. That's what the "relevant" part of "Radically Relevant" is all about.

# about

# *not*

When it comes to the target audience, too many people focus on demographics. But in branding, we care more about psychographics: categories of people based on attitudes and values rather than physical attributes. What does your audience need functionally? What do they need emotionally? It's an exercise in empathy: Put yourself in your audience's shoes and let their needs—not your preferences—drive your brand decisions.

**It's not easy. But it is core to the Radically Relevant brand.**

# you.

# 3.1
# Hey, good lookin'

**CREATING BRAND ATTRACTION**

One day while scrolling through Instagram, I was targeted for a hair-loss product. And, confession: like many men my age, I'm in the midst of a hair recession, and the algorithms somehow knew it.

The post that popped up wasn't cheesy or gimmicky like you would expect a hair-loss ad to be, and it caught my attention. The packaging and style of the brand was clean, stylish, and slightly masculine. In fact, even the name was catchy: Hims.

I thought, "Wow, this was created for a design-minded, sophisticated, slightly hair-challenged man, just like me." I investigated a little further, and—after it passed the sniff test—selected an option that would autoship monthly to my house.

When the package arrived a few days later, it was beautiful: like a treasure chest of good design (and hope for my hair). There were snug-fitting containers, a pleasant opening experience, smooth finishes, and a contemporary type style. Eager to brag and show off my new purchase, I presented it to my wife, like a first-place trophy in online shopping.

As a trained holistic practitioner, she was curious about what was inside these tiny hipster bottles. So she googled the ingredients.

Turns out, it was generic Rogaine.

My jaw dropped to the floor. I didn't need Rogaine! Rogaine was for men from the '90s in sweater vests and khakis. But it was true: The Hims product was the exact same medical treatment, just rebranded. Hims saw a hole in the market for men like me who are concerned about hair loss but care about design and don't think of themselves as aging. Hims used beautiful photography, messaging, color, and type to sell a group of products that wasn't all that special behind the labels. And they had everyone fooled—even a sophisticated branding guy like me!

Hims (now Hims & Hers Health) has seen incredible success with its approach. By 2021, they had grown to 600,000+ subscribers and reached $272 million in revenue.[12] All while simply improving the appearance of products that, on the inside, had already existed in the market for decades.

# That's the power of attraction.

Businesses that embrace design generate 32% more revenue and 56% more shareholder returns, on average.[13]

# But what if you're not a brand-new brand? What if you've already been around the block a time or two?

In addition to the fixed guardrails discussed in the previous chapter, your brand guidelines should also have flexible systems that are designed to evolve. Your brand name should (hopefully) never change. But you may have a new campaign slogan every year. Your logo and core brand colors should be consistent. But you may introduce a new illustration style or secondary colors every once in a while to shake things up.

# Visual Systems

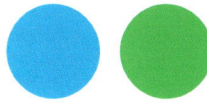

**Bold**
**Semibold**
Medium
Regular

**FIXED**

Primary Logos
Primary Colors
Typography

**FLEX**

Photography
Trend Colors
Iconography
Illustrations
Patterns/Devices

# Think about your favorite Netflix show.

Let's take *Stranger Things*, for example. In the first season, the creators introduced the essential elements: the storyline (a boy disappears into an alternate dimension and his friends have to bring him back); the key characters (Will, Eleven, Joyce, Sheriff Hopper, Mike); the setting (1980s Indiana); the genre (science-fiction horror); and the tone (spooky, nostalgic, funny). These elements make up the core identity of the show.

In the second season, the creators added a few new characters (Max, Bob Newby) and an updated storyline (Will is back, but now the monsters are out to get everyone) to keep things interesting. Similarly, you can boost the attraction of your brand by changing out the flexible assets in your kit of parts. Sprinkle in a fresh campaign message, some secondary colors, and a new graphic pattern or illustration style. Just like a great Netflix series, in order to remain relevant, you have to bend and flex with the seasons, while staying true to who you are at your core.

Consider Nike. They can be flexible with their assets, because they've elevated the meaning of their brand to such a high level that it's transcended their products. It's not just about better running shoes but the feeling you get after a run (whether you just edged out a competitor in an ultramarathon or finished your first neighborhood 5K). From the 1980s to the 2020s, the core elements of the Nike brand—their name, their Core Message ("Just Do It."), their "swoosh" icon—have remained the same. But year after year, they use new celebrity endorsements, ad campaigns, technology, design, and more to keep audiences engaged—and attracted.

# Beauty Tips for Your Brand

❑ What leading brands are also in your audience's world? What can you learn from their brand voice? What can you learn from their design choices?

❑ What is the driving mindset for your audience? What do they emotionally need? Find ways to message and design to that more than anything.

❑ Your audience is the hero of their own story,[14] so how can you reposition your brand as the guide or helper, rather than the protagonist? One simple trick is to turn your "we's" into "you's" so you're speaking to your audience, and not just about yourself.

- ❑ Attraction is all about nailing your value proposition. So ask yourself: Why should my audience really care? Once you've zeroed in on your brand's best assets, think about how you can highlight those assets first in the consumer's mind.

- ❑ Outsourcing to a firm or agency can be a great shortcut to attraction, but projects can sometimes go off the rails when the focus becomes the client's personal taste. In these situations, try to tell yourself: "I know what I think about this, but what does my audience think of it?"

# 3.2
# Keeping your brand's promises

**CREATING BRAND DEVOTION**

## I'm convinced that if Darth Vader were a brand, it would be Comcast.

For those of us old enough to remember cable TV, we have horror stories of taking a day off work and waiting hours for the Comcast repair technician to arrive. In 2010, Comcast attempted to distance itself from its negative reputation by rebranding its high-speed internet service under a new name: Xfinity.

Xfinity released a slick new logo and tagline, and promoted the new brand during some sweet, sweet Olympics airtime. But the name was the only thing that changed. Your bill is still wrong. Your box still breaks. Your service still goes out. The only difference is that now when the technician finally shows up two hours past the appointment window, they're wearing a red Xfinity T-shirt instead of a blue Comcast one. Instead of investing millions in launching a new brand, the company could have just fixed their customer service problems.

Brand attraction is important—no doubt. But beauty is only skin-deep. You can do everything right in this book, but if you don't deliver on the expectations you create for your audience, it will all be for nothing. Because the best branding can't buy you brand devotion. Instead, you must build it over time, by consistently and repeatedly doing what you say you are going to do.

During the early days of the COVID-19 pandemic, the world was facing many hardships. My family was faring well, but after a few weeks locked inside a moderately sized house with three young kids (with immoderately sized personalities), I was about to lose it.

One thing that brought me comfort: Trader Joe's gluten-free, dairy-free cauliflower gnocchi. (Stop judging me—I was gluten-free before it was cool.) I had a hankering for that lovely microwavable miracle and decided to risk life and limb to acquire a stash for my freezer. A trip to TJ's (and away from my house) was in order.

I made the 10-minute drive in less than eight, because in those days, the streets of Atlanta were virtually empty. So were all the Kroger, Publix, and Walmart locations I'd been to since the pandemic began. But once I pulled up to Trader Joe's, there was a line wrapped around the building. Of course, I took my place at the back without a second thought.

**When your customers will wait in line for 30 minutes just for the chance to buy a pasta that's actually a vegetable, you've figured out devotion.**

"I heard somewhere that a brand is a promise, and a good brand is a promise you actually keep."

I heard somewhere that a brand is a promise, and a good brand is a promise you actually keep.[15] But it's hard—maybe even impossible—to get everything right every single time. Especially if you're a brand that sells both products and services. (Getting one or the other right is hard enough, but both?) That's why we start with the most important elements: the unforgivable aspects of what you promise that, if broken, will greatly hamper your reputation. We call them your "get-rights."

We worked with a nonprofit that promised a safe space for visitors to recharge, reflect, and rethink. But to do that effectively, there were a few things they needed to make sure they got right. We defined those as:

- Serene Settings
- Next-Level Hospitality
- Experiential Programming
- Passionate Volunteers

Imagine trying to reflect on your life goals and personal relationships while not being able to find the food hall. Or being on the verge of a breakthrough and the leaf blower interrupting your train of thought. Additionally, they needed experiential programming to truly unlock how their guests viewed themselves and the world around them.

As another example, we helped position a B2B HR technology company as "the high-volume hiring technology using insight and delight to exceed the demands of the world's leading brands." That is a fine-sounding statement, but if they didn't get a few key activities right, it would be meaningless. In order to be "insightful" they needed new product offerings that integrated into existing HR platforms to aggregate data. In order to be "delightful," they needed to nail the applicant user experience and interface for mobile platforms. Additionally, they needed to sunset offerings that weren't built, at their core, for hourly hiring.

When you think about your brand's positioning (as defined in the chapter on distinction), what implications does it have for your product and services? How does it double-click down to your customers' experience? What must you get right for this positioning to be felt and true in the market?

Devotion is where the rubber meets the road with your positioning. You can't just say it—you have to operationalize it. Then you must continue investing in those get-rights for your brand positioning to become—and remain—a reality.

# Otherwise, you're just looking at Xfinity 2.0.

# How to Get the Get-Rights Right

- ❏ Define your get-rights. Choose just 3 to 5 to focus on. They could be related to product quality, customer knowledge, or operational excellence. (The fewer and better defined your get-rights, the easier it will be to start seeing improvement.)

- ❏ Measure your success in each key area. Use simple surveys to collect feedback from your customers, donors, and/or other stakeholders on a regular basis.

- ❏ Identify areas of weakness and create a plan to address them. These could range from UI (user interface) updates to new customer service models to employee recruiting efforts.

- ❑ Empower your team to make these corrections.

- ❑ Repeat.

## 3.3
# All systems go

**CREATING BRAND ALIGNMENT**

Brand devotion goes hand-in-hand with brand alignment—because you'll never deliver on your brand if you don't have buy-in from executive leaders, as well as the boots-on-the-ground staff who are the face of your brand.

In the previous chapter, we talked about how Comcast's service operations are just as much a part of their brand—probably even more so—than their name or logo. So how do you get all these moving parts working together?

## The secret is alignment.

If you've ever stayed at a Ritz-Carlton Hotel, the moment you step out of your car, an associate is there to take your bag. From the CEO all the way down to the valet, everyone is working toward creating a hospitable experience. (In fact, their motto is "We are Ladies and Gentlemen serving Ladies and Gentlemen.") So what happens if the CEO has a vision but can't get the employees to execute it? Or perhaps more commonly, what happens when the creative director has a vision (for more brand control, attraction, or distinction) but can't seem to get on the CEO's radar?

It's one thing to come up with a great idea—it's another thing entirely to successfully and consistently execute on it across the organization. For this to happen, someone inside the C-suite needs to believe that brand is important. They need to see and feel the power of it. They're the ones with the authority to elevate your brand position to the strategic planning level and make sure that everyone in the organization knows what's most important to deliver on. Otherwise, you're swimming upstream.

A great example of brand alignment is Ellevest. An alternative to traditional Wall Street firms, Ellevest was founded as an investing platform built by women, for women. To understand their audience more deeply, they first conducted a study asking women what they thought and felt about money, investing, and the financial services industry. Then, in order to align everyone in the company around the average customer's needs, they gave her a name: Elle. From top to bottom, every employee at Ellevest now has no doubt who they are intended to serve.

As of the writing of this book, Ellevest has raised $53 million in Series B funding and has 350,000 Instagram followers.

Alignment pays off.

While the effort must start with executive leadership, the real test is getting everyone aligned at the staff level. Education and discussion can help. We once worked with an architecture and engineering firm whose work ran the spectrum from award-winning skyscrapers to tire manufacturing plants. Their brand felt like a bit of a hodgepodge, but we realized that everyone in the organization had something in common: They were approachable, down-to-earth people with brilliant ideas. So we landed on the positioning, "genuine ingenuity." They loved it! At least those on the side of the business who created iconic city structures loved it. But the ones handling the less glamorous projects disregarded the concept because they didn't feel like it applied to them.

This alignment problem had the potential to undo all the hard work we'd done together. So we held a workshop where we discussed how to apply the brand positioning to every area of the organization. While the tire plant wasn't as shiny as the skyscrapers, the engineering solutions they'd created to prevent negative environmental impacts were definitely ingenious. Once this group saw how the brand story applied to them, they began to own the positioning in a big way.

# Summarizing your brand strategy on a single page can help keep it shareable, digestible, and top of mind for your staff. We call the single page a brand brief.

# Brand Brief Template

### BRAND POSITIONING

What do we want to be known for? What is our radical relevance?

## We are the

[first noun category]

## that

[area of distinction]

### BRAND PURPOSE

Why do we exist? What story should we tell beyond making profit?

## We exist to

## BRAND PERSONALITY

What is the distinct character and tone of our brand?

### Attribute
_____
_____
_____

### Attribute
_____
_____
_____

### Attribute
_____
_____
_____

### Attribute
_____
_____
_____

### Attribute
_____
_____
_____

## AUDIENCE PERSONAS

Who are we ideally creating the brand for? Not at the exclusion of anyone else, but who matters most? What are their needs, desires, and fears?

### Primary Audience
Value Proposition

_____
_____
_____
_____

### Secondary Audience
Value Proposition

_____
_____
_____
_____

# Getting Your People on the Same Page

- ❑ Before engaging in a branding project, create a roadshow presentation to socialize the need and the opportunity. Make sure the CEO is on board, and make sure the problem to solve is crystal clear.

- ❑ Then get input on the new brand upfront. Hold workshops and send out surveys to really understand the level of alignment (or misalignment) in your organization.

- ❑ Make sure brand is considered in the next iteration of your strategic plan. Hold brand workshops for key leaders, where you introduce your positioning, show the reasons for it, and discuss how your brand story applies to each of your unique offerings.

- ❏ Map out your customer journey so you can visualize the full experience a customer may have with your brand. Then ask, "What does it look like to deliver on our positioning at every moment of that experience?"

- ❏ Tie employee performance back to the positioning. If your brand promise is all about kindness, and yet you have a high-performance leader who berates the employees, what does that say about the authenticity of your brand? What steps do you need to take to restore it?

- ❏ Encourage your CEO to champion the brand purpose, position, or story from the podium. Make it a central theme for all internal communications.

# Section 4
# What Now?

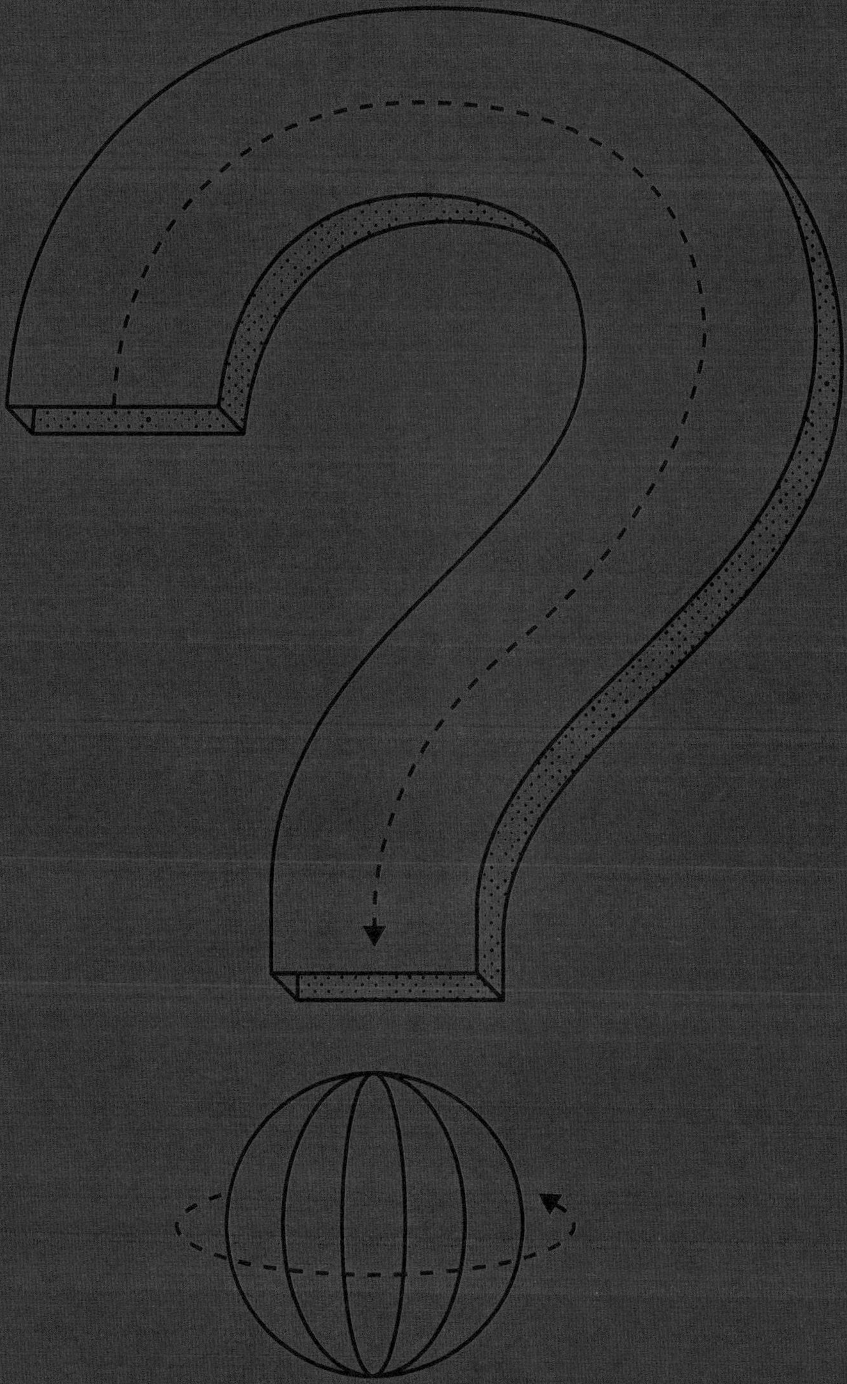

# GET TO WORK. THEN KEEP IT UP.

If you started this book looking for clarity, hopefully you now have a solid understanding of the Super Six, as well as some actions steps on how to improve.

First, you've got to get to work. Then once you've found success, you'll need to keep on getting to work to maintain your coveted Radically Relevant status.

Start by validating some of the hunches you gathered from the assessment with more audience or consumer research in order to truly understand their perceptions about your brand. If you need support, internal buy-in, or alignment, share the assessment with others on your team. Show it to your boss and see what their take is. Then discuss. How much change does your brand really need? What land mines do you expect to have to dodge along the way? What are the real problems you are trying to solve?

Then determine how you'll measure the success of your branding endeavor. Are you looking for increased awareness? Stronger employee recruitment and retention rates? More leads? More sales? Having a clear vision of what success looks like will help you stay focused throughout the project.

Branding is more of a marathon than a sprint. It takes time. I like to say it's the positive version of death by a thousand cuts. More like…reputation success by a thousand interactions. (Rolls off the tongue, doesn't it?) You don't have to bite off everything at once. Instead, pick the most critical brand issue facing you right now—as well as the one you have the best chance of success with—and start there. Likely, that will look like your lowest-performing of the Super Six.

All things being equal, start with devotion. This category is the most basic in terms of value exchange, because if you don't go above and beyond to serve your customers, then you'll have no business or mission. Until your organization is equipped to follow through on its promises, any branding effort will have the lipstick-on-a-pig problem. Once you've finished, address the next most critical area, and so on.

# "Branding is more of a marathon than a sprint. It takes time."

Hopefully, a few years from now, you'll find this book in a desk drawer and realize you are now a Radically Relevant brand—in the upper echelon of all organizations. (Or maybe you were one of the lucky few who had a Radically Relevant brand to begin with.) Congratulations! But before you pat yourself on the back and rest on your laurels, take a moment to consider one more thing: Your brand is a bit like your GPA. One bad exam can tank the whole thing—which is tough for growing brands. Because the more you grow, the more complex your brand experience becomes, and the more opportunities there are to bring down your GPA.

Remember Comcast? They have so much to get right: the technology of the box, the lines in the ground, the huge customer service staff, the scheduling and wait times, the technicians, the billing, and so on.

# No wonder they're continually flunking their brand GPA.

To maintain long-term brand value, you have to put systems and processes in place to consistently invest in your brand. You have to keep studying, keep showing up to class, and keep acing those quizzes day in and day out. Here's a model for how to do that.

# First, always have a finger on the pulse of your audience's needs.

Never assume their experience matches your intentions. To keep up with their evolving expectations, you'll need to create a continuous feedback loop, whether it's a simple pulse survey after every transaction or a Voice of the Customer study commissioned every six months. Define what you want to measure, based on your get-rights, brand attributes, and positioning, and craft your questions accordingly.

# Second, keep an eye on your competitors.

Follow your archnemesis on social channels. Set up Google alerts. Did they create a new offering? Did they refresh their core message or go through a big rebrand? Commission a competitive audit. Watch for any big moves your peers are making, as well as brands you look up to and the industry at large.

# Then, let your findings fuel projects and initiatives related to improving your brand.

This is where your flexible brand identity assets come in. Plan a series of rolling projects in which you explore ways to keep evolving your flexible assets, based on what your customers are saying and what your competitors are doing. Maybe you find you need to push the brand voice a little, tweak your illustration style, invest in new custom photography, or craft a new core message. Maybe now is the time to clean up your product or service architecture. Branding is like painting the Golden Gate Bridge—it never ends. You don't have to implement every single idea that crosses your desk, but scheduled projects can help keep your brand top-of-mind and ward off staleness.

# With any changes you make, continue to reeducate and inform people at all levels of your organization.

Look for ways to keep brand top-of-mind with everyone from veteran to intern, and from sales and marketing to operations and HR. Conduct internal training continuously to make sure people know what the brand is, why it matters, and how to use it.

All this is a lot of work, sure. But it's work worth doing, because it's what your audience and the market think about your company. It's your reputation. And at the end of the day, the brand isn't for you—it's for them.

If you can determine the ethos of your brand, find what makes it great, and get everyone aligned around that, then you really can scale and get everyone headed in the right direction. Whatever barriers are keeping you from that Radically Relevant place, I have no doubt you can overcome them. You can build—and maintain—a brand that people want to follow. One that creates wild fans of its audiences and gets used as examples in books like this one. It won't happen in a day, but if you follow the advice in these chapters, step-by-step you will get there. You'll gain the wind in your sails and begin to enjoy the positive momentum of a Radically Relevant brand.

Even though we're at the end, really this is just the beginning. The important thing now is just to get started. So go ahead. **You've got this.**

# Acknowledgments

This book is the result of many years of collaborating, sharing, and being inspired by the brilliance and generosity of others. First, I'd like to thank my wife, Kelly, for her patience, love, and support for many years. This book is a result of your commitment to me and our family. Secondly, my kids, Banner, Abby, and Ryder. Your creativity and imagination inspire me every day — do not ever shy away from doing hard things.

I'd also like to thank my business partner, Craig Johnson, for his trust, vision, and friendship. I'd like to thank Alina Wheeler for believing in me and helping us see the future.

I'd like to thank all of the Matchstic team, partners, and friends who contributed to and collaborated on many of the ideas represented in this book: Devin Bambrick, Brittany Blankenship, Jonathan Bolden, John Bowles, Dee Boyle, Dustin Britt, Ken Burnhardt, Tracy Clark, Mitchell Ditto, Pamela Henman, Jay Holden, Kenny Isidoro, Jill Jeffries, Sean Jones, Jonathan Lawrence, Brianna Mears, Sarah Melnyk, Meghan Murray, Sarah Gail Neibur, Jason Orme, Jim Reese, Ashley Williams, and Danielle DePiper Wilson.

None of this would be possible without our fabulous clients: Adam Bain, Brandie Barton, Gilles Bazan, Sean Behr, Abby Bradley, Ashley Brown, Andrew Caliendo, Chris Carneal, Luke Christian, Dwain Cox, Pouya Dinat, Jennifer Dorian, David Farmer, Carlos Gonzalez, Joshua Harrelson, Christina Hill, Angela Hilliard, Lee Hogan, Alicia Hunt, Nate Hybl, Jonathan Karron, Tim Keane, Andy Levine, Bryant Malone, Derek Maloy, Beth Martin, Haley Martin, Layton Meng, Kim Miller, Michael Mithika, Patrick Murray, Stephen Murray, Reed Nyffeler, Bill Palmer, Frank Patterson, Ric Peeler, Michael Robbins, Sherri Daye Scott, Elizabeth Sholes, Richard Simms, Jeremy Steffens, Tony Sundermeier, Deanna Traa, Eric Weir, Amanda White, Chris Yadon— thank you for trusting us with your brand.

Designed by Brian Paul Nelson
Co-written and edited by Acree Graham Macam
Printed by Standard Press

# About the Author

Blake Howard is co-founder of Matchstic, an Atlanta-based brand identity firm. For nearly 20 years, he has focused on helping growing companies level up their brand identity by being Radically Relevant.

Blake has led brand launches for hundreds of projects, spanning a broad range of clients, from global heavy-hitters to ambitious start-ups poised for growth. The most notable of these brands include Boys & Girls Clubs of America, Chick-fil-A, the City of Atlanta, International Justice Mission, Publix, and WestRock. His work has been featured in *Fast Company*, Bloomberg, and *Designing Brand Identity* by Alina Wheeler. It has received recognition in Graphis, *Communication Arts*, and Brand New.

Blake has taken the stage to speak on brand identity best practices and creative courage at AIGA Atlanta, Brand New's First Round, DesignThinkers Toronto, HOW Conference, and MODA. He also brought Creative Mornings to Atlanta, founding the local chapter in 2011 and hosting it until 2021.

Today he hosts the podcast *A Change of Brand*, about the world's most loved consumer companies and their rebrand glory, drama, or disaster.

# Endnotes

1. Source: https://www.uspto.gov/dashboard/trademarks
2. Source: https://www.charitywater.org/about/financials
3. Source: https://water.org/documents/231/Water.org_2021_annual_report.pdf
4. Source: https://companiesmarketcap.com/tesla/marketcap
5. Source: https://www.forbes.com/sites/forbesbusinesscouncil/2021/08/20/building-brand-recognition-through-your-content-and-bi-tools/?sh=116451863894
6. Source: https://fashionunited.com/news/fashion/patagonia-tops-reputation-rankings/2021051739965
7. This strategy was made famous with Apple's focus on the education market. Xennials, ever wonder why your school's computer lab was full of all those weird Mac computers?
8. So much of the thinking in this book is indebted to others. This framework, which we use at Matchstic, was inspired in large part by Marty Neumeier's book *Zag*.
9. Source: https://www.healthcarepackaging.com/markets/neutraceuticals-functional/article/13296355/cocreator-of-method-and-olly-disrupts-the-first-aid-category
10. It will be interesting to see if Intuit's acquisition of the email brand will sop up some of its quirky personality.
11. Source: https://d2slcw3kip6qmk.cloudfront.net/marketing/press/webinar/The-Impact-of-Brand-Consistency-Report-New_Cover.pdf?submissionGuid=89838c0e-01f6-478a-9f55-e2e2234638e7
12. Source: https://www.fiercehealthcare.com/health-tech/hims-hers-2021-revenue-jumps-83-company-expands-retail-collaborations
13. Source: https://www.mckinsey.com/business-functions/mckinsey-design/our-insights/the-business-value-of-design
14. See Donald Miller's *Building a StoryBrand*.
15. Google tells me this was Mutar Kent, former CEO of Coca-Cola.